[re]turn

Kristen Lang

Kristen lives in mountainous country in north-west Lutruwita/
Tasmania. In her writing, closeness and connection combine
with a beyond-human view that celebrates ecological continuity.
Her collection of poems and photographs, *Let me show you a
ripple*, was self-published in 2008. *SkinNotes* (Walleah Press) and
The Weight of Light (Five Islands Press) were published in 2017
with the latter longlisted in 2019 for the Margaret Scott Award.
Earth Dwellers was published in 2021 by Giramondo Publishing
and was one of 20 books longlisted for the international Laurel
Prize. The book was shortlisted for the Tim Thorne Prize for
Poetry in 2022. Kristen works in a voluntary capacity as a flora
and fauna surveyor in the mountains near her home.

Endorsements for *[re]turn*

This is extraordinary work, environmental poetry with a difference, pieces so rich in detail, experience, imagination and wisdom that one must read them slowly, aloud if possible, to savour and absorb each line and sentence. This is not theory, not preaching, not rancour, this is true love and knowledge of place. Lang takes her readers by the hand and, like a lover, introduces them gently to the mysteries of earth. It is voices like this that might just lead us through the purgatory of our time.

DAVID BROOKS, POET, NOVELIST, ESSAYIST

Kristen Lang rambles through the wilds of Tasmania recording bats, tracking echidnas, sampling soil, cataloguing plants, and counting the uncountable abundance of the world. These are the poems in which she stores her harvest: ravens and wombats, trilobites and tardigrades, slime moulds and whale sharks – they're all here. But Lang is no mere naturalist. *[re]turn* is a field guide written by a visionary, the music of a mystic with stars in her veins and the sea in her voice. Her poems defy the fall, repair our rupture from ourselves, and promise that the boundary between us and the world has been illusory all along: "And what am I? Helmet orchid, heath dragon, / a fringe of rain, long-tailed mice and copepods, / the lattice of their waves in the coils / of the heat in me, and my warmth, too, / in their layers." This book's great triumph is its vindication of a world already whole, an order that accounts as much for stars as star-nosed moles. And so saturated are Lang's lines with wild places that they leave their traces on the reader. After handling these poems, I find their pollen on my fingertips. I brush their leaves out of my hair.

MICHAEL LAVERS, POET

This poet's work is my constant companion when travelling overseas, an uplifting reminder of our entanglement with the world even when I am caught up amid the business of our cities. I feel such an affinity with how she weaves together both the macro and micro, the vast and the intimate, the poems alive to the ties between. Through her words, yet again I find myself reconnected to what I value and treasure.

ANNE MORRISON, ARTIST

Kristen Lang's *[re]turn: love notes from the mountain* invites us to (re)open our senses to the natural world we inhabit, which inhabits us. The lines between selfhoods in these poems do not so much blur as meld. Lang's informed and passionate engagement with the environment is deeply reflective and alluring, at times reshaping human language to pay homage to other forms of communication. Shimmering against the surface of exquisitely detailed imagery is the persuasive entreaty – beyond self-preservation or moral obligation – to care.

JANE WILLIAMS, POET

Kristen Lang

[re]turn

love notes from the mountain

UPSWELL

First published in Australia in 2026
by Upswell Publishing
Perth, Western Australia
upswellpublishing.com

Upswell operates in the city of Perth, on ancient country of the Whadjuk
people of the Noongar nation who remain the spiritual and cultural
custodians of this beautiful land. We acknowledge their continuing
connection to country and express gratitude to elders past and present for
their strength and creativity. By extension, we acknowledge also the land
itself and the vast, enriched relationships within which all life is embedded.

ISBN: 978-1-7637331-9-0

A catalogue record for this
book is available from the
National Library of Australia

Cover artwork: Montage of works by Troy Ruffels
courtesy of the artist and Bett Gallery, Hobart
http://www.bettgallery.com.au
Cover design by Chil3, Fremantle
Typeset in Foundry Origin by Lasertype
Printed by Lightning Source

To stand with one's arms raised, hips gently
dancing, in the flex and release of all the Earth's
muscles. Nothing belongs to us. Everything has its
threads through our bodies.

And if not arms and hips, dear life, then
whatever is the equivalent.

"everyday I hold a piece
of everything"

Jill Jones, *Wild Curious Air*

Contents

love us

strata

i)
Mustering into my hands the loam she was /
is made of, my 9-year-old self / 12-year-old /
20-year-old. The ground, I explain, her roots

are fused to – sand, a little clay, pieces
of the moon. She's oblivious a while longer,
busy with what the do-now verses across

the ever-bigger rush of the city tap
into her skin about who she could be but isn't.
The loam, I say, but she doesn't hear.

She gets the awe of the weight of it –
the jut and buzz of the river, the winch
of the stone-creased horizon, the miracle

of peacock spiders, snout beetles, blue-tongued
skinks. But not herself, still in the making,
new in her imaginings. In the half-sketched

blueprints of her want, the rock, air, rain
of the Earth no more than a backdrop.

ii)
I hold the loam where I am, digging in
while the 9-year-old drips her touch as if

from a distance. Though she's not a visitor.
So close to believing. Earthling, she'll say,

sun suckler. I stand where the river pillows
over flow-shaped stones, days

sifting their hours through the rub of the water,
the moss verge feeding into its rhythms.

I try again. Walking. Upstream. In the web
of the universe. Each star's campfire

in the pupils of my eyes, each flare's crackle
in my tongue. The eye a barn owl's, the tongue

a forest bat's. Shingleback. Emu-wren. The same
seed of response. The river narrows.

Its flung light shimmers in the dark, in the run
of its chatter – *here   here*, I say, the loam

sinking into my palms and the sky, too,
in all the cells of my body, *there is nothing*

else to adore.

briefly on the mountain

The human I live with
is across the water, holding the hand
    of his father who is dying –

I and the dog we slip
loosely into calling "ours"
    are here beside the mountain.

And maybe place
is never really the contour but the climb,
    the steepness pressing the touch

into time
the body remembers. His father moans
    against the pain, against, too,

the morphine, the torpidity, wanting
some other journey, a pulse more
    ocean

than his own – air and lift
and allure, beyond lying
    in the fade of his warmth.

I want his son
this same way – the litheness
    of the river, how the dark inside the stones

resonates on the plateau, how the wild trees
bend over the paths of my walking. To know
    his weather through my own,

the tangle of us
under the wind-swept branches of the forest.
    We are distracted

by ourselves. The moment reminding us
the hour is still arriving – death
        comes / and goes. He calls me now,

asks how we are, says
barely anything, relief   slow-danced
        in the arms of loss.

The dog and I
step into moonlight, the blue-white
        boulders of the mountain

drifting into the night. How the horizon
is just a game, the son, like the dog,
        spinning towards the day a while,

my pulse
brushed by the falling
        of eventual rain.

between stone and light

You would know us by trunk
and leaf and light fall,
    slow-knit formations in the tides
of the Earth's atoms.
        You would know
    this wrinkled skin
under branch, over root bulge,
    lipped curves in the trunks'
        long ridgelines, peeling
    into seams and hollows.

The sky becomes us, the air
        feeding our pores. The rings
            of our flesh
        tattooed by the sun. Stone dust
            turns to soil, the soil
    to stone /   root
                and bone /   seed
        and cry /   and wing tip.

        You would know us
    as Pencil Pine, Mountain Ash,
Lilly Pilly. The bristle-tongued birds
        mopping nectar, clawed feet
                gripping
            beside the bugs
and the moss, this bark-
        coloured tree frog, the tree skink
            bearing its young.

        You would know us
    by your in-breath. The stick-
            and-ball child's mark
                on the thin

pressings of our wood.
Rain-thirst in our canopy.
Wind
loosing our scribblings
into its swirl. Know us.
No less – love us /
love   us
in the unquietness
of your world.

bedrock

The stone knows at heart, of the microbes
tucked into its grains, that they too
are a part of it. Laced, like the trees
and the flatworms, with its solidity, the birds
moving as shards of its wind-caught self.

For aeons it has leaned
into the act of speaking – earthquake
and avalanche, and with a polish
of its vowels, the grunts and hoots
of its embodiments. In the silk of its spiders'
threads it has spelt the name for each
shade of darkness, each edge
of green-tinted light.

It longs for poetry,
that the infusion of its stoniness
might bear, beyond trees and moss
and spotted-tailed quolls, beyond mayflies
and geckos, the pivot of its dreaming,
the crux of its own unfolding.

It thought the cadences
of the flowers would be enough,
the exquisiteness of the songbirds' calls,
but still it leans. A tongue
more articulate than its rivers, a voice more
abundant than its soils – how the stone

pushes out until it cannot
recall its own beginnings, shaping the air
with the hauntings of its new designs –

gods and nations, the jangling
of its coins, one and at once divided –
here, says the stone, *I am.*

In awe of its own making, it fills
each human mouth with the tales
of a seer, propels them with its mineral
hands. On and on it dreams, driving
into the belly of its hunger. Its night sky
cluttered now by the lights
of its myriad eyes. And the sprawl
of its reach hurtling into thin-lined
amalgams of its stone-braided thought –
copper and gold and cobalt.

The poem begins –
a seed in the dust of stars
dripping its molten touch, its voice
pouring its potency, the resplendence
of its force, through the husk
of its stony self.

[re]turn

we are falling as always
this time through the fire-floods
a brush of hands sharing
heartberries, palm prints, pieces of shell

I am taking you into the forest. Dear J.
To that tree we like. As if you are real.
The truest of my lovers.

Moss crawls on the vertical folds,
the whole base undulant, year rings
nudging girth into a shiver of sky.

Do you see it? We stand too with its brother,
hollowed into edge like a peeling of light,
ferns leaching their emerald. Our human

skins, my skin, J, in the bark-rubbed
breeze, as infused as the foliage, arms
in the air and swaying. *You,* we say,

placing our hands on the trees inside
as well as beside us, dripping our vowels
into leaf litter through deflections of sky, *you*

are beautiful, outrageous, our tongues
in the tang of their leaf shadows and the moon
resting its hooks, waiting for darkness.

we would risk each other's eyes,
flesh becoming wood becoming air
and the wind diffusing us,

curling us into its scent as if each
border were crossable

Beyond the forest, in the slow-gathered
creases of the valley, the first
foothills, J. Already I am climbing.
You tell me the age of stone – late cambrian,
early ordovician – yet under our feet
the churning, half-molten core,
and the stone tides, J, waves
travelling here through the mantle,
my step-step feet in their pulse.
And yes, I'm climbing alone,
again and again up to the plateau,
but you, in the forest, the town, the city,
are in the same slow-breath rise
of the ground, ebb and stone-melt flow,
dust on your soles. And because
all of it moves, eruptions
through the waves themselves,
in the mountain rock there are shadows
etched by the sea, high above the ocean,
shell ribs, a hint of coral pressed
by my fingers, the moon-earth
tug leaning through our bodies, juice
from the mountain berries in my mouth.

heathmyrtle, ground parrot,
quoll prints in the frost-
bitten chill, you and I
in our unpolished faces, still
squirming out of the soil

There are rufflings of light through the stringybarks,
splinterings under a blackwood, the tree-ferns' russet hairs
peppered with glow, taut-tendoned fronds
hustling their furry spines into the shadows.

The wind is riotous. Cold-dropped onto wood-
and leaf-rot, unused, I find the nest of a pink robin.
Beautiful, J, cushioned with fern hairs, moss walls
a vivid green, the tight lip capped with lichen pads,

plaits of silver web coaxing the curve. All the poems
have been written – the bird, the nest, the punch of it
in my hand, the voltage of its emptiness. New,
rubbery heads push from the palms of liverworts,

their green sex pumped into the coiling air. *On*, I say,
stumbling through the gaps in my hearing, a flatworm's
silk-bellied sheen, amber-striped in the leaf mulch
as I try to listen. And you, J, is the shrike-thrush

still at our window? The tap, tap-flit dance as she sings
into the glass, the keen pitch of her pulse lingering
in our bodies, filling my ears even now.
Or the blue of the blue wren, brilliant

as he jabs, leg and claw and wingtip, cobbling his mark
under the bottlebrush – is he there? My footprints
are in the soil behind me. How I fit, so often,
my steps into their curves on my return – a confused

kind of erasure, a wanting
perhaps for weightlessness.

> *some of the clouds are hammocks*
> *we would rest in, yet the day*
> *tumbles forward*

We drive home from the hunt-n-gather –
six bags plus an esky – and leave the car
parked with the bonnet up to deter the rats,
stockings on the side mirrors, the two sparrows, one
scarlet robin still alighting. We place squares
of melt, a sweetness on each other's tongues,
chocolate-lust in our lovemaking, the touch
of Ecuador, wet now in our mouths, the long, long
history of cacao beans absorbed into our cells.
We're arching our backs between the beets
and sweet potatoes, sugar snap peas
under your shoulder and the fresh yeast
slow-breathing in its remnant chill,
the chew marks on the brake cables
merely, we say, superficial.

> *a silk-velvet sigh – the crater rim*
> *teetering into avalanche, the vertigo*
> *spinning its grip, how for a moment*
> *no-one clings to the sides*

When we wake, it's to the sound of a kookaburra
slapping its kill on the roof iron. You say the noise
has stirred the dragonflies under your skin, and under mine
there are caterpillars. Three-hundred-and-sixty-eight of us
under the covers. We phone in ill, spending the day
lakeside with your wings and my cocoons.
We pull beer cans, plastic bottle tops, a piece of old
clothesline, one stiletto, a flip phone, three copies of
Avatar on dvd from the shoreline, one shopping trolley,
which we fill to the brim. We take samples of the brown-
green water into our bellies. And wait awhile.

pieces of beak, pieces of root
and tail and lung, whole kinds
of creature, how for aeons
the factories in our tiny cells
made none of it – no bone or wood,
no shell… we kiss each other's lips
as if they are animals

There was an eagle in the paddock, J, do you remember?
Close to the house. It swooped onto a tease of dorper wool,

nothing there but dregs in the wet, winter grass, you and I
staring from the verandah. When I think of it,

I imagine the wool wrapped round my toes, if only to feel
the weight of him – claw grip, beak edge, the suck

of his inhale. At the time, we were awed by of all things
the size of him, and with the sound in our ears

of news reports, shot guns, we could see
the hole it would leave, his pivot point impossibly gone.

We watched like ravens, the skin tight round our shoulders.
And in the spring we planted stringybarks, mountain ash,

hundreds
and hundreds of them.

at the tips of the fingers
of the functionaries
in the offices for felling
trees – entire
forests of them – small
fruits emerge, tiny blue

umbrella fungi, puffballs
and branching corals;
they open their mouths
to rain clouds and the spidery
hues of grevillea flowers,
nothing but pinks
and powdery yellows

Sunlight catches the chic
logo of the carbon app
we've installed to save the planet –
for each item scanned
it shows a line turning
green or red from this
or this point of departure,
an emissions guide, the line
ever arriving – coffee beans,
news feeds, tomato seeds…

What does it mean, J?
The screen says
there are billions of us.

in the agal bloom
we're holding our breath,
trying to see through the water

We cut through our left wrist bones, both of us, the skinsack
horribly roughened. We leave the hands to dry a little,
skin shrinking onto bone. What the hands cannot do, we say,
makes room for the flea beetle, cuckoo wasp, velvet worm,
even the wombats and the dunnarts. It's a kind of promise. I think
of the handfishes and whole swathes of grassland, greenhoods,
blue-tongues. Mine is in the garden, a shy eyebright

between its fingers, knuckles pushing up under the thrust
of grubs and millipedes. They rot of course, or erode, vanishing
in the flood of the day's atoms.

I let it rise, a word born
in the cave of my heart muscle,
squeezed through my ribs
and so compressed it holds
through the mercury, burnt
fossils, paint solvents, on its slim
ascent into the void, the sun
in a breathless sky – breathless,
that is the word.

Shall we stay awhile?
Up there on the mountain, J.
The peak's blue jags
in the brittle frill
of the everlasting daisies,

crumbs of them in the wind.
Shall we stay? Dawn
till dawn, and dawn again,
speaking in stone
to the day stars, night stars,

ribbons of cloud,
fringelilies round our hollows.
The same
sliver of sky
will enter our mouths. If we sleep,

our pillow will be the air itself,
the scalloped edges of the chill-
hardened shrubs

nudging us into position.
And when we wake,

in the pink-pearl
blooms of scoparia, the sundews'
silver nibs, a fresh
bronze glow dressing the myrtles,
we'll know, as if it's new,

the soak of us –
rosella calls, the gaze
of currawongs, the tarns'
dark inversions.

> *we are falling as always,*
> *mountain frost, bird nests,*
> *lungfuls of sky, dust*
> *becoming stone and the breeze*
> *running its trace through us both*

Through me, J. To the north, smoke catches the westerlies,
the fire distant, though there are scars further down
along the ridge line – cracks finer than hairs

in the fire-baked ground, like an echo. A palm press
and whole slabs skittle out of the dry perch
of their brokenness, black-white shrubs

crumbling into the soil. Are you there? The smoke-
hazy moon spins over all of us. A raven caws, wing
and light and leaf-tip, the sky-body embroilment

also our own. Your name, J, let it be aeons
old like the universe, let it be open
like the arrival of time.

we barely believe, we say,
how in love we are, kelp forests
shading our blood, fireflies
by the lakes of our tongues, the sun
right here in our bodies

everyhill

Where the goat's white curls
are swept apart, catching the gusts
punched out by the stone-pocked ground,
the russet roots of her hairs become apparent.
The child has a name for the goat,
and the goat, too, for the child, a scent name
she feels for with her whiskers.

They are climbing a hill made stark
by its treelessness. Crimped summer flowers
nod at the trail's edge in a half-rubbed shade
of yellow. They barely know each other.
The goat's lips stretch for an air nibble
at the child's thrust-out chin – the scent
is of mint-flavoured toothpaste, a mustiness
from the cupboard the child's hat was stowed in.

The child believes the goat is also the world,
that her gaze carries everything, centuries old,
the glistening of it all in the silver-blue
of her eyes. The child feels it. The hill as well.
The mash of bonds gripping in the shifts
of their layers and nothing to hold
one thing from another.

Were the child to record the moment –
the climb, the day, the weight of the Earth's
aliveness – she would say, "rock shapes protruded
from my fingers", "leaf veins sang continuously
of the stone." The purple-jawed orchid at the crest
of the hill was already in her marrow.

walking the rainbow

Light spills across a fray of sky
into the shower of rain we are walking in,
Luke's hair lank now with slow
accumulation, a few beads still in his fringe.
He asks if the rainbow has a pulse,
light catching the drops in turn
as they pass the precise angle of his gaze,
a tiny jitter in its hold. I ask
about the air between the drops,
the push and flutter, our lungs
breathing the ripples of the rain's
gentle falling, and the impact, too,
as it lands, the dance of leaves, the high-
pitched singing of the grass.

Are there presences, he asks, plural,
trillions of them, or just the one?
The rain, the sun-caught shivers of it,
carries on regardless. Either, I think,
and both. I recall to Luke, as still we step,
a woman I knew, *Ingrid*, how I love the name
because of her. I recount how she liked
to think of God as being in-between
e v e r y t h i n g and how,
to catch a glimpse, she would ride
her tight-wheeled bike, unbelled,
fast down hills, the wind
scrawling through her hair its own kind
of language: *fwoosh*...

It matters, he says, that we bear witness:
the tree, the river we adore, the days
we bind into togetherness, the *in*
the *between* gifts to our hearts. He and I

in the carved-out traces of ourselves
though perhaps, flung out of our own
entangled ways, we would touch, too,
a little of all of it, drifting as we are
under the lit-up clouds. The sweep
of the unselfed divine and at once,
the particular life, this
honey in the mouth. We are here
with the sun on the rise, the rain
clearing in this wave-point
expanse, alive with all our chatter,
two birds leaving their songs
behind them and the frogs
starting up again
as we pass.

flux

I hazy the sky with my dreaming
      backbeat   *hinge*   *hIpsway*
a bird too on the guy rope of her tiny pulse
    the two of us
            eddies   the air riddles through
    in its wavelets, light   becoming
           forest   becoming
  wombat   *canary worm*   *yourself*

I'm dreaming of dunnarts. White feet
        in the dark. One   wrapping her paws
round my finger   like she never has.
          While my toes   dig   down
  to feel the microbes   breathing
    under the ground, deep
        in the cracks   of stone, one
  new cell   per century   beating but
        not quite a heart.

You and I   phenomenal in our thin
      descendant membranes
    root-coil   *river-swirl*   *dawn*
        becoming day. I am
land crab I am   crow claw in the clutch
    of feeding I am
        desert pea, afloat
    in the flux of being.

what the girl hears in the forest

With their sky-grip, in the wrench
of the Earth's orbit, are the just-hatched
trees. She can hear them age, feet hunched
under moss and rock and fungal webs,
the lichen feeding its nibblings into their hunger.

She knows, in the stitch-*un*-stitching
of all the Earth's bonds, life
and death and erosion, there is herself as well,
hung in the sprawl of it.

The weight of it as she listens. The ferment
over time – tussock moth, leatherwood,
the creaking of the forest, rivers finding the sea
and the sea finding the gulf of the galaxy, galaxies,
stars swerving into stars amid the thrum
of the black holes, quintillions of them.

Rain trickles into cells, breath
into cloud. The shape, the shapes *not*
cradled in her thought, in the tease
of the moment's swell.
Moonlight
          on a puffball's
                    spores.

below the summit

The pandani have scattered
mid-step in buttongrass, necks wrapped
against the cold. Torsos a brief illusion.

We sit listening to their patter.
Centuries-old migrations woven
through the slow-tumbled stone –

they are not, they tell us, the only ones
on the move. Ridgelines
jagged with sea shells, molten eddies

thrust into the light, rucked and crushed
and crumpled, dust swimming
in our arteries – we too

are this shift of ground, our bodies laden.
Seams of riverbed, my lover says, filaments
of grassland, collecting fish swerve, claw prints.

The fish, I say, bear in turn the imprints
of the city – metals, plastics, why
are we surprised by that? Not joined

by the Earth's currents but of
the elaborate whirl of us, flow lines
in the tug and buffeting, chasms apart and

still entwined. Pollutants and salts and light
trickling through our cells. We have built
walls across the paths of trees. Cut

through the feet of mountains. The pandani
rustle their scarves, or their tongues,
call them anything, but listen:

the breeze
on our skin as we pass, pricklings
through the sharps of their leaves,

the angled weight of the crags, beyond
the self's deflections and as near
to the Earth as we've been / as we've

always been. Lips kissing the sky.
Time bearing our bones
through its travel.

the barest distance

I calculate the mass of water
falling off the mountain – now, and now,
with each step of my climbing. The mass too
in the clouds to the west, the rain's tilt at fluidity
steepening in their greying hues.

The river is vertical. Trees have grown and gone
and grown again in the time of its tumbling.

Across a gape of stone, the ripped waves
plummet both above and below me,
the spur I am on protruding
into the midpoint of the mountain's
cut-away. Dustings of abraded rock
enter the air, as always. Sunlight, with the breath
of birds, the breath of skinks and of spiders,
of myself, enters the shrubs, caught
in their green palms and stitched
into the closeness of their limbs.

Half my life I have lived
on the river that begins here. And still.
Less than belonging, I arrive. Writing it
into my skull with these small words, this
"green", this "crease of stone", this
"uphurl in the gobs of water" – how I am here

and am not, am flesh like the plants, bone
like the crags these old roots wrap around,
though they do not bend towards me
and I cannot hear their thought. At the edge
of the overhang, the shrubs and I, the morning light

behind us, are thrown onto the fall's far wall,
our shadows on the sheer cliff
below the plateau. Each the breadth
and height of the other, my one raised hand
waving, like the branches, only I

am against the wind. My shutter clicks.
Keeps me there. The lens lending its truth.
My likeness the barest shift
from the shades beside me,
warmth from the sun seeping
into my shoulders for as long
as the image holds. Shadow and light.
In the mesh of my cells. These words,
made of stone and shrubs and of the swoop
of water, trickling
out of my mouth.

the splendour

a song of swirl and atoms

How all of it works – the winter light breaking
into the blossomed snows of spring, the mountain
etching its stone, again, across the horizon, the low sun
rising into the seed of summer's heat, and you,
all the motes that make you, all of us, every membrane,
every kindness, every war cry ever wrenched
into existence, every raindrop making its way
into each living cell, every breath, every story we tell,
every footstep, all the billions of newborns like ourselves,
hundreds of thousands of years of us,
and beside us, the den diggers, nest makers, algae
and coral feeders, lichens and sun-triggered flowers,
slow-carved out of the sea and the ground, the quolls,
honeyeaters and echidnas, snow skinks, dung beetles,
the millipedes tracking their lives round our own,
and the wide, enormous time before life first formed,
the aeons of each and every place in the making, all of it
wrapped around us – the bones we share, the soil.

We cradle our forgetting, polish a sense of separateness,
wearing it like a crown, while the Earth's intimate web
trickles through us, photons to the flux of the weather,
one ephemeral dawn to the entanglements of all of time,
the thornbills, white gums, orange-bellied parrots,
and us, inside the mesh of it. All of it. The aurora
redding the sky with its sun-swept flares, each
flickering heart that has ever passed where we stand –
spider, wombat, wattlebird, the first note ever sung,
the first dance, and the one even now that hip-sways
in the hunger of your spine.

Everything. That ever was. And all of it,
right where we are – the wedgetail feeding its young,
the potoroos and the pygmy possums in the crucibles
of the land, the tree roots, the impossible fruits
with other trees inside them. And I
am connected to you, and to the moths and mosses
and platypuses, simply by being here, simply
by tugging from my still-warm chest
the will to care, this place ours

only so much as without it
our names would be weightless.

Bloodpull. Earthscent. Leafburst.

Planting our tenderness in this place that is our pulse.
All we hold and are held by, as old as the universe,
as new as the next sound you will utter. Under moonrise.
Into the hail and wind. In the stillness. Now, and for as long
as it matters. Ourselves in the glorious chance.
Let the sound you make

be the deep, slow hum of your affection.

maybe birds
trill too against the smallness
of their bodies

how to be human

Hold, the poem would say,
how the Earth holds – through and without
borders. Give more than you can spare

to the way the trees curve the sky
into their cells, their cells into the sky,

into hyphae, into groundwater, leaves
glowing their limes and jades into the air rivers
of the birds. Would it say that? This poem?

Etched onto pages cut from the trees'
encircling years – we forget

they were poems already. It would say,
stay awhile, with the owlets, brittlestars, pine seeds,
the astonishment of their unravellings. It would say,

pay heed by threading light to pulse
to rainfall, speak as if the self were at once

wren and yellow gum, mountain breeze,
hovering among the spiderlings, in the melt
with the snow fleas, travelling in the treehoppers'

patter. So many lives. The wrappings of the world's
intricate veins. We're tapping our memes,

prettying up our faces – tropes of eyelashes, lips,
lacquered hair. The wide, inexpressible
swarm of us. What is it the trees

might exhale from their leafy mouths – *touch
-of-the-sky-soil, water-sun*, meaning ourselves

as well, each quantum spin throwing its web
across the boundary lines with immunity.
How to be human, how to be river, how

to be turtles lured by the town's bright lights
away from the sea. The poem buries the "h",

abrading the "m" into tendrils of admission.
How to be "u", "n" finding the beak of a night-
parrot, "a" in the lift of a hover fly,

the breeze jumbling us up into shapes
we might learn to care for. How

to be human. A decline in the birth rate
sending the frights through an exorbitance
of accountants, though we know

the Mars ship can't take all of us.
How to shed our verbal skins. How to be

diatoms. How to be grasshoppers. How
to be mineral, a flexure in the sky-rock dome.
How to move and know it muscle and bone,

and air and ground, and every breath of the weather.
The poem says: *listen,* as it always does. And because

it's not implied, *don't,* it says, don't *stop* there.
Never stop at the listening. It's never
the end of things. Only the beginning.

The worlding we've done, because of us, the reach
into our touch-of-all-the-others – the blue

whales starving in the airless heat of the slowed,
buckled currents... *Everything we take
comes from somewhere.*

Would the poem say that? Would it need to?
The damaged Earth prophecy has arrived – do or die.

It *doesn't* say that. It says: how to be first
responders – here in the river, says the poem,
or the wetlands or the forest, the open plains

or the cityscapes. Leaf vein, wingbeat, even
in the AI hatchings of our post-human songs –

the love, too, will be wanted there. The poem
says the world sifts through the core of us, the core
is already the world, lifting it

on our palms, all the atoms of our blood, all
the flagella, the ocean vents, the dark matter.

We try living it like we believe we belong,
the biome becoming the self, dust-
and world-sized, aeons deep and hung

in the tremor of the universe, as if that
could be enough, the fleet echoes of our hearts
nudging the air with their shimmer.

buttongrass

for vombatus ursinus

one of the stones
flings a stumpy leg,

then another, crossing
over the way
we have come.

I trundle back
to the paw marks,

the texture
of her pads, trenches
for the claws,

and remove
my shoes
and socks till I'm
barefoot –

ice shards
in the chilled
softness of the mud.

raising the bio

I am not of emu totem, not of shield bug
or goanna. And so I make
the weave again from scratch,
though it's never that, peeling apart
the glitter.

I say the flesh restoring its cells
in the city of my body
brushes leaf and fin as far away
as time has seen such things – all
I have been or will ever be
in the stern and tender trade
of biotic flow: root and bone, beak
and broken shell. Like yourself.

And when we dig
our fingers into the sea's
unfathomed floor, the current
nudges the krill, the whales,
the fishing boats through the narrows
of our capillaries; heart valves
full of sky, sky lights, satellites,
the wide, hard fragility of the land
pressed again by our wanting.

Such a mass of humans now.
Vivid in the night's rave.
The swarming of our noise. I drag
what I am through the self's
shallow mirror for what the arc
of the day might reveal in us. I am not

of koala totem, more moving as toys
than in the heat of the living. I am not

of mountain ash or silver gull.
Not either of the parklands
or the virtual greens
screening the forest trucks
in their thousands from each
town's gaze. We've slipped
too far for that to hold.

No. It's taken awhile, but: *you*
are who I turn to, you
with the night's yawn in your eyes.
And no-one asked the emu but
please don't mind. Blood
and skin and gristle: *you,* dear friend,
these filmy words in our mouths,
the moon-sun
jostling the stone-tides, the seas'
hustle of waves
sucking the ice, the un-
treed parrots in our hands.

You of the pulse we share, of the air
we pass around, of the sun's
perfect distance, the water
falling again from its clouds, each
of your gestures, every pause and desire,
and no, I do not raise you but
pledge under your weight and touch my own
in-love attentiveness, that we both
might emerge into the world.

You do not need
to love me in return.

But love a little.

And as I climb
onto my roof to mark
the revelation, your likeness
held to the sky and the sky
covering everything, perhaps
it is your turn.

A banksia down to the left of me,
a spinebill lending his tongue.

You may choose
any and all of us.

currawong

She rolls on her back,
beak tossing the twig her feet
have played into the air,
the game a way to coax
the surge she feels
through her muscles,
the rush in her young feathers
still confined.

The bird behaves
as if to know a thing
is to have it erupt inside her, song
pouring her day into a shape
she will learn to recognise,
the torque in her wings
gathering and the flight-
imprinted sky
enlarging in front of her.

She throws the twig,
struts across the ground,
her high-shouldered
shock at where it lands
fooling no-one.

please,

the wings are powdery,
the colours cream and walnut brown,
and on this ground, white-
speckled amethyst, like eyes, rimmed
in black and floating on a disc of ochre.
At the thorax, fine hairs flecked
with pollen, ink-line feelers
wavering in the air. Please,
I would rest a butterfly
on the lift of your tilting face, half way
from your lip to your attentive eye.

Stillness. A foot
probes. Edging. Onto cheekbone.
Your skin
listens – catch
and release, the petite
step. How your cheek hairs
stiffen at the tremor, tiny hooks
in the dendrites of your nerves.

Black legs, glossy like
candied threads – you count
each press, each brush. A slight
breeze as the wings spread. Then close.
Like blinking. You scent, in a whisper
of the creature's heat, the faint
trace of its hours – light
and air and such
bright petals, how the widest
of stones slope gently
to the lushest flowers, the sweetest
of nectars.

Until the wind shivers.
And the six feet let you go, swept
into the weather. Your eyes lock
on the coloured wings, the rickety wave
of their rhythm. And perhaps
all the cocoons you cannot see
stir in their slumber.
Rain gathers over hilltops
and does not plunge – you lean
into scudding cloud.

A butterfly
taking off with a trace
of your marrow. And because
the smallness is large in you and the grip
tight in you, and because
you cannot keep such things,
you decide, with your lips
brimming, to carry the quiet
charge, like a bud into the world,
and you kiss

the cheek of another. And the kiss
is light and at once deep.
Without want or need. Catch
and release. This touch – how it's
beautiful. Awkward.
The two of you breathe
and the weather folds through you
and your bodies
jolt in the tug of being. A butterfly.
Please, I have kissed you.

porous

The peak veers from solidity – light, in its hurtling
speed, plays into everything, probing as if to inhabit
yet always becoming. It's heat travels through her.
The rock, too, sifts into her slightness, crumpling
the slip of her shadow, feeding its ragged slant
into the muscles of her body.

Rock against sky, sky against rock, a counterpoise
dense where she stands, each edge voicing the other.

She can feel the knit and dissolve. Her feet
on this high crest, arms spread above the fall,
the cobweb of her steps tugging into vertigo, rock
and flesh and light in the spin of the Earth. Her small
escape into the real.

recalibrate

The diameter of the bullet is that of a man,
loaded onto a jut of rock a sheer thousand feet
above the valley. Aimed only at himself.
He doesn't fall. Two thousand feet. He climbs.
Three thousand. His grip-laden hands unroped,
drawing the stone into his chest, its worn,

wrinkled skin against his own. If it knows – each
molecular shift, each crack filled by his fingers –
the reply is stillness. Push-and-catch, lock-and-rise.
The seconds seeping into stone-time, wrapped
around a trillion dawns, his stretched muscle
feeding into the glide of the Earth's orbit.

The man trickles upward, pouring his insect steps
into his airy trail, swerving gravity through his spine.
While the wall. A wrench of rock. Pitted
and creased. Gnarled crags crunched over furrows.
Molten pools and ripples bent now into fissured
folds. While the wall. Slowly. Slowly weathers.

I listen for his song. A shadow clutching at stone
in a tissue of sky. So I hold. Threading heartbeats. Push.
And rise. Clean. And uncluttered. *This* matters.
And *this*. In the beautiful world. Breath
sucked through a straw of bone. May I fall,
when I do, wrapped in the wilds of our living.

love on the radar

Some say it spills out of the ether,
a heady, unbounded force washing over us,
     stripping us of our veils
          and leaving us bare, our feet
filling with *everypath*, the Earth's unpinned
     horizons in our fingers.

     Some say it cannot hold
     to any named thing, sifting into being
          beyond the tales the self tells
of just a morsel – "who", we say, "who is the loved
     and the lover", while the love
               swells again through the stones
          and the air and the rivers.

You call it grace, like a star
     amid the clutter, and perhaps
          the noise is its strength,
     how the reach in us, the hard
climb, climbing again,
          and climbing, lends us the touch
     of its shimmer, never wholly its witness

     …remember
how the sky might still arrive in us
          as we descend.

     Some say it coils in the Earth's spin,
     through the atoms time has passed
          into molecules of water,
     through forests and to deep-sea
          corals and whale songs, shavings
     of the universe in the tendons
          of our chests. And as it folds

and unfolds, "I", we say, a shiver of it
curling from our tongues, "I
        love you".

So we become, as if
out of the air, ourselves,
        drenched in these vast melodies –
"here", says the tune, "and here",
with the lungs of birds, with the buds
        of trees. And with our breath: "do not
pass", says love, "do not leave if you cannot
        hold me inside you, carry
the care in you
        like it matters".

Dawn. To dawn.
The fragility. Love
        again please
                erupting on the radar.

her actual size

for Clara

She would enter the river of scent left by the night.
With the trees, we shared the strokings of the sky,

fibrils of our heat braiding around the branches.
A fray of pulse from the birds that passed, the lizards,

the possums in their hollows –
who can know

the boundaries here? The congress of her being
crossing my own, junctures in the crowds

of the world – how missing her
shears tides from the sea.

the lake

We arrive at the shore
awake to the body of water, mist
bleeding the breadth of it into our skulls.
The caress. The breeze. The stone-rimmed
weight of it.

At first she says
I am the lake and *she* is the arrival,
but in truth she has come with cross-currents
in her chest, pebbles in her mouth,
some of them ghosts,

and I too carry reeds within my bones
and fingers of stone for skipping,
the shoreline taking its shape
from the confluence. The prickling
as the waves

lap around us, wattle blooms
spreading from her palms. Our feet lift
from the ground. And the glide, she says,
is what light must feel,
finding its leaf after so much

timelessness. The mist
barely rises. Trees nuzzle the roots
of their reflections. And we wait
for the mountain rim, untethered
in our brief-sweet

immersion. The Earth
and our flickering selves.

phase shift

In the view from Andromeda
even the buds of the purpleberry,
even the tiny ones,
move in the spiralled dance
of an orbiting,
orbited galaxy, the one
you liked to tell me was "our own",
fox-trotting in its night jewels
round the magellanic
clouds.

I called you the moon,
how you nudged
further out until
circlings of another kind
might be born of you,

a swaying of Venus, perhaps,
or bridgework
to another universe,

a tug in the solar winds
lending some other moment.

You need not return
nor were ever   going to,
the tilt of your spin glowing
in the tango of the dark,
and the dust
settling here inside the poem.

the bird of longing

The birder-songwriter is saying,
about the longing, about the mysterious
hue she stops for in car parks
and under the limbs of stripped-bark trees,

about the lure she does not or
cannot name, how it must
be listened to,

the despair
as well as the wakefulness,
the hint of elation.

She means literally – this sorrowful music,
over-and-over ear worms of ecstatic sadness.

She crafts a melody, a guitar's
bitter tenderness, the rent
and reach enough to stitch
what she feels into the drift
of an almost vision.

She presses into the bruise,
her lyrics strung
across the compass of her hunger
and yet

arresting her with their narrowness.
Such shavings of the Earth. How her sounds
become and unravel her, the pungent scent
of their promise fraying
under the weight of her humanness.

She is adept at mimicry – wren calls,
the warblings of magpies, mopoke hoots. Flight
a lament, though her tongue's
tiny suck of the rag she has soaked
with her fancy unfurls from her as she sings.

In her want,
each note carries
to the horizon. Winglessness
an emphatic refrain. And maybe birds

trill too against the smallness
of their bodies. Spreading the wisp
of their staccato into the air.

She borrows shapes beyond her own,
gathers the epochs, the first fin
and tree root, claw and bright-lit flower,

her fading tune the flimsiest of additions,
a fringe-echo
in the all she belongs to.

Belongs... the *being* of her *long*ing,
how she hovers in the rift of it.

Bird-writer – she cups her palms
round a life half-feathered. Parrot-beaked,
scrawny-necked, the tiny head packed
with sound blooms, patterned
beyond remembering. She tucks
the puckered skin into a box-nest
for wintering in. Protected

for a while beside the others: a pair
of pardalotes, an injured owl, a goshawk.
Pulling her heat round their shoulders.

They tell her the song, sky
filtering into their locked-up gaze,
lies as much in the branches
as their bodies, and in the rain
and the sliver-thin wings
of the insects.

As much, she thinks, in the too-heavy
pockets of her marrow. As much
in storm winds and the promise of dawn,
frost dripping its gleam into the turbulence.

She's listening
at once to the cloth she drapes
round their night times,
to the hooks of their feathers, the air-net
of their tiny barbs. She knows now,
it's in every chord, she cannot live
without them. The self
sung entirely by the world.

fffffooooooo whaaa
fooooo
frip frip

roots through the clefts of time

In the night, the trees approach
and pass as creatures held
in the glide of the Earth's turn,
their inky rise in the starlight
sending the rush of the planet's travel
into the upbeat of my walking, each
crevice of my awakeness.

The land slopes, creased
into twists and channels, stream-flow
in the folds of its muscle, my feet
crossing the shallows. Dank soil
sheds its scent, my palms marked
as well, in my grab and pull,
by the stones that protrude here –
boulders and broken shards
thrown about by ice and sun
and age-spent tremors.

Dawn plays through the blackwoods,
glossing the gums, the tree ferns
hunkering down on their shadows. Light
steals through the water, filaments
and scraps of glow.

At a hollowing in the hill's
furrows, like a thumbprint
pushed into the tilted ground, rock
jumbles its angled self into a pile
as sky-drawn as the trees, outcrops
stacked on jags, the rough
ridge and towered slant leaning
into lichen, stag ferns, green-
covered branches.

Thick-barked wood on a trunk
broader than myself bulges
around the stone, midway
in the outcrop's rise. It's a ledge
I can climb to, lipped
by the clutch of the tree's
contours, the trunk still ascending,
morphing from its press
into round again,
skin ruffled by the join.

There's a flush of want in me.
That I too might reside here. Or here,
along the edge where this gnarled
blackwood emerges, roots
nowhere visible,
the rock's fissures etched
into its grip. Dark, weathered limbs
lit with cushion moss. Branchlets
splaying as they twist.

I move as high as the stones
will take me – leaf tips
in the sun-woven air; small
citadels of emerald from the spores
in the bark's grooves. And so
doubled is the hill itself,
there's no descent – a rubbled step,
broad-leafed vines and eucalypts
bearing on towards the mountain.

As if unsure of its level here,
a thinner tree, but old, as grown-on
as the clambering ground, keeps
to the horizontal, lower than my chest,
stretching east before its arch
dips down and back

into leaf mulch, its fluid swerve
circling it at last into its canopy,
spreading its sparse umbrella
barely above my head, root
and reach in the touch of my hands.

And this before the sun
has quarter crossed the day's
fleet inventions. What I've seen,
scarcely a sliver. These trees,
fusions of my slim-stacked
years in their elaborate lives –
shoots and veins, the push
into stone, under rain,
the slow shaping of the air.
And beside them, faster of tongue,
scrambling through the hour, some
part of me learning to be.

the spin of leaves

i) *under tree fern*

    the giraffe-neck tilt of its hairy hide, bearded
       with moss and filmy ferns, how it
      sways, wobbles under her palm, as wide
as her body in the lively air – she's soaking in leaf glow,
        sassafras greening the sun
            into a canopy of lime,
        the trees' roots visible round the ferns
mottled bones, frond under branch, wind
       engulfing the girl with the light's shattered ripples

ii) *mountain*

    old gums thin   as saplings   crammed
    with mountain-storm   all-this-place
    in their limbs   the dry-jagged   crags
    the frost   on snow, the moss-   sunk
    stones   the night   behind-the-blue   leaning
    into their skins   their pinks   and
    greens and yellows   polished   into silver

iii) *song*

      the tips of their branches – *stirrup anvil hammer* –
burst with alchemy, sculpting the shades of green – *we try but*
    cannot mimic them – what they hear
           of the sun's flares, some
        echo of it, audible in the play of the wind

iv) *of an age*

down the mid-trunk, how the bark and wood curls
in and apart, like lips, the mouth
opening, the bared tongue breaking into buried
chants – rot and nests and fungi spores,
spider webs, the tree turning its core
into a part of the weather… *caw*, says the raven
caw   caw, then silence, beak
in the crumbling, through the soft-bodied grubs

v) *spent*

all rift now   yearning   desertsoil andtoomuch   sky   greensong
stripped and broken   inhispalm   myrtle burl   scraps of waratah
the coupe   deepcut   this   branchthis   trunk discarded   inhis
hand he can sell   saladspoons   letterholders

vi) *new wood*

the roots are slim, slight   hardnesses
under her feet   under the soil   the lift she feels
as she inhales   an airiness   that as
they carry her   is the hatch   too in their
twists and greys   of such   bright wood
clean and   brimming with colour
a mauve haze patched
with salmon   silver bellies   faint
lines of lemon   leaf chatter
in the breeze   the sky
beyond the woman   gazing on

vii) *growth chart*

the shrub's tips and branch stubs bash and whip on the gum's
heavy trunk   wind scars, tender on the thick-haired bark
the shrub   wiry in its count of squalls, inching   a little higher
etched   in the tree's circles

viii) *lingering*

odd-lit   gaps in the forest   stark white trunks
not dead but clinging   a twig sprouting   russet
the cracks   held   by what   leaches still
from the roots' remaining tendrils   are they home?
in this   and this hollow   a hint   of movement
small   feet   tiny mouths   blooms of fungi
a green-blue   head-feather   sunlight
on the rungs of dust

on visiting Dr Bell

A cosmos of moons and suns, near
nothing in the vastness, taut

with what we cannot see, the slight
sway of the Earth, like blue-green

wings, shimmying, Jordie says,
in the yawp of the universe.

The man building frog homes in his yard
where the frogs should have been

but weren't, has just such
a shape about him. Pieces of

nebula in his eyes. He hands to us
tree parts kept millions of years in the ground,

the wood-no-longer-wood
having emerged in his excavations, black

as if burnt by time. We note too,
in the corners of our watchfulness,

the atoms not in the tree but here
in the pond and the pond weed,

in the bitterns, also ourselves, in the drink
bottles and the cars we have come in,

in the unformed (Jordie collects
cocoon husks for his future child), the unborn

arrangements yet to follow,
expressions of this

and so many stars. We know
we are all – trilobites, tardigrades, the first-

ever galaxy – as old
as each other. He tells us the wood

turns flaky when it dries, that it's
drying as we hold it, a weather-front

in our palms. He wets the wood,
submerges it under cloth while we talk

about the state of the environment,
the deferred, official response, the air-

tied hands – Jordie's painting
whale sharks, woylies,

dugongs and tree frogs
on their fingers – the want in us

cradling nothing but
everything in the balance.

west

After the purplestars, the beaded
sundews, the twisted carpets
of wind-crimped fagus,
wizened trunks on the king billies,
after the pink of the crags has silvered
under the clouds of unhurried rain,
smooth jags rising out of the lakes
in this claw-gripped surge
of ragged land, after the day
has darkened, and because
of the unravelling, the dust
of time across the terrain,
less of me has returned
and I am more because of it,
adrift, off track, unnamed.

desert shadows

Rumico says there are dragons,
her fingers enfolding pieces of their split
and twisted hides, our steps bearing our bodies
over their haunches – crease
and crack and protrusion.

She is not the first to think such things.
The Arrernte living the ebb and turn
of so many stones, river beds, hollows,
blood routes through the millennia.
The tourists now, too, like ourselves,
wanting the grip of it, to be here
as if the land were inside us. And beyond
the humans, beyond the blink of us –

hook and fur and feathers,
claw prints and tree roots, even the flight
of dung beetles crossing the aeons.
We breathe. We breathe and a sliver
of these veined and rippled rocks,
cubes and cauliflowers, camel humps,
cliffed and slabbed and looming, an in-breath
of this weathered ground
somehow carries us. Demands of us
that we hang whatever lies at our core
against the sky. The lift of it from our chests.
Like a homecoming. Bone
finding its dust. We are saved

by five small birds – budgerigars slicing a path
through the air ahead of us. The stone as if
releasing us, for a while.

the swimmer

There are flowers that open twice. He thinks
especially of magnolia, how it shifts,
changing its form, changing its form, one

bloom after another. He feels the husk
of the words he speaks huddled
round the rawness of his body. Strips

gently beside his car, his day's stretched
hunger for the water's pulse
luring him into the sea. The clamour still

caught in him will rub into the wake-now
pummellings of the breaking waves.
He waits for it. The self he holds, thinks

he knows, propped up on the foreshore
with its scaffold of mantras. The sea
buffers him from his trappings, the moon-

besotted tide peeling him from his other orbits.
He listens. An as-if fledgling heart
in the salt-hung skin of his witnessing.

Inland, he's a swimmer of trees, travelling
through the narrow roads to where the trunks
hug into highland winds, ridge

after ridge rippled in a hunkering
of moss and heath, the snow-
toughened saplings shaving the air

for the buds of their leaves. Storm-ripped
limbs dangle from the canopy. Thin reefs
of seed grab at the sky. He strokes the light

along a lift of bark, the wave peaks
of the forest's crowns bearing him upward,
at once outward, as far as the horizon.

Again, there is no divide – the points
of the gums' leaves, the dark rings
circling the years, leaf-fall, sap flow

flooding now into his cells, the will in him
like stars among the branches. His un-
frameable love wholly what it is.

Opening. No more than a shimmer.

stringybark

the small girl asks
could she be granted
treehood... that she might
photosynthesise into the cool
of the afternoon
stretch her toes into the mesh
of the soil and not need
to answer the question
of how the trees
might be yet protected
from ourselves.

I am seven or eight, standing with my feet half
buried in the dry debris of the eucalypts, their grey-greens
perched beyond the house I had thought was home.
My child's gaze

hooks round their stringy-barked arms, their long,
wooded exhale, forestfuls of air and light contoured
into time's clear trace – leaf and gumnut, root-coil,
becoming in-breath, ribs, lungs. That when I trip

back across the paddocks, through the grass blades'
crush and quiver, my spine is swayed
by the inclusion.

I am thirty-six or seven, learning tree roots, the bonded
sprawl of their alliances – hyphae, bacteria.
The trees I would still become are drinking the sky –
old, bent myrtle beech between

the mountain stones, peppermint gums
shrinking their bark around the crumbling of their trunks,
their hollow cheeks curved into possum dens,
parrot nests. The child in me –

bones full of rhizomes and orb spiders, leaf-miners
in my palms. The slow-fluid shapings. The fleetness
of the hour.

cider gum

We are all of us light.
The camera gifting its thimbleful
onto the canvas. None of us –
leaf, bone, river – any different.

In the moment itself, the sun's
sharp stream enters our skin
as it pours as well into tree branch,
bird song, the escarpment
playing its rush against the weather.

It breaks now into this slight touch, the man
with the lens tilting his eye just enough that his ear
too can hear the chatter of its infinite colours.
His probing hands. Lips stung by his closeness.

Frame after frame
of its trace while the leaves
shake him back into their flow.

Light falls, too, into darkness.
Tree rings. Leaf rot becoming soil. Days
becoming memories. The trees eclipse
the span of us – the slow riot of their forests,
the hem of the sky inside them.

They are not
human, these trees. Why then
are we in love with them?
In the man's gaze, stark
spidery forms crawl
across the highlands – he is here

for the still alive among
the skeletons, the loss
hung in his silence.

Cider gums, *wayalinah*, ruddy-pink
mottlings on the bark, silver-greys
matching the sky, the clean
buds in the older leaves' rattlings.

Where the limbs are bare
his reach is for their grace, step
by step in the teetering
of his strength, as if the weeping
might end their vanishing.
He would bleed for them. Soaks
his quiver of time into the land
and paints, with his images,
the unquiet claim

of their forms. The light in them
aeons old and echoing
what in truth he knows
he belongs to.

double horizon

I send Kyle to walk the next
mountain over and we talk
to each other, in-stride as we step
our respective paths – heath, ants,
boulder stacks, his urn gum, my
stray myrtles. At our peaks, we're so
counter travelled in each other's
eyes, his lemon boronia, my
pineapple grass, his mountain rocket,
my matcurrant, creeping pine, his
cushion plant, our feet could be on
either line, his mottled cloud pierced
by my blue sky, our precise
locations confluent
in the stitch marks
of our waking.

swell

A torn hue,
the battered flesh of the waves' deep shade
bleeding the tide onto the canvas.
Nothing in me waits, dipping this rain-
pervaded body into the turbulence,
the sea a tangle of time I touch as it writhes
into the space that holds it – brushstroke, frame,
the angled lights of the gallery.

What it feeds in me! The salts of my cells
knowing here how the ground turns under us,
the fluid roll of the stone stretched
a little moonward. I forget the fleetness,
reaching my palms into the sting and suck
as if the seconds might last forever, the wall
gracing my thirst with its relentlessness.

If we scoured the unpainted dunes – old
surf boards, bottle tops, the scattered histories
of shells, waftings of down – we'd find, as well,
words left by the passings of others. "Aqua",
"muka", "maambanal", "home". Plucking them
from the fish bones and food wrappers
and sighing into their hulls. They speak

only in shadows. As the smallest of ways
of falling into the green-becoming-grey,
the painter painting a gap we might
slip through, the surge of it
larger than all of us.

the blue it takes

i) sidelong at the water

   a falling curl engulfed   like a backwards sigh
bell sounds   of juggled stones, slow   *S*-curves etched
      in a tangle of silver   a caught leaf
         in the judder   in the rubbings of sky
      cloud-hung blue
         scribbling the river...

ii) drawdown

   the gumnut   in its rain of seeds
        sunlight   crimped into the tree's
     recurring hold   a resolving of   sky
each leaf   knitting into the air at its side and
who would have known – THE BLUE IT TAKES,
    stem-then / vein / eruptions-of /
   bud / root-matter / spider-breath / skink-
     tongue / random   hairs / chest-feathers
/ bone

iii) speaking only to the trees

fffff
   fffffooooooo whaaa
      fooooo
         frip frip

  fffffffff

     scuh   scuh scuh scuh scuh

iv) breath

what if the air could be seen but the birds   were invisible
pock marks where their beaks opened   breeze-hemmed
flutes of song   wing-spirals   brushing our skins
twining   into our mouths

v) earth tide

nothing is still – jags
    and faults and sea-filled rifts
                in a sigh   of solid ground
            breath marks of the moon
        swayed   by the sun, the weight, too
    of the sea   and of the air
        all of it
                strung   into tides in the stone's
    swell, half   a body length   in its movement
            each   step, each
        hill climb, street crossing, each
    moment's pause – wavefronts
                of push   and pull, the ground
        tugged in its flow
                        our anchor
            mere
        gossamers of thought

vi) burn

molecules *pht* of cellulose *tutut pht* lignins *swut-swut* in the tremor
pht/stigit-takata ig\NItioN/*fwuuuUu* sttigit **HAA**aaaahgh rip /*pht phwwt*
fwuuUtututt sky skyfulls of *hooOstigg/tut gaaaah--flikflifli***smoke**
/*pht pht-shwooOm pht htht*/h**Ot** crumpling *hhaaaahh/flit* wh**O**oo-gtgtgt
smoke and ^*gtgt stigita/stigita/sucsucsuc* sucked *shooowaaAh* air *shttt*

mesoscale

The water chitters, bustling
under our torch lights.
We're dropping blackwood
flowers into the eddies.
  Drift
        and turn,
              s t r e t c h
      and spill,
flow curling
into slow-fast – s l o w
like an amoeba.

None of the blossoms
travel on. Caught in the stone-
scented flick and roll
of their ragged circling.
How the tumble of waves
fills the estuaries
is a conundrum, the current
kicking again through its twists
and returns.

At sea, the eddies are marked,
side to side, as large as islands,
wriggling their ways
into the weather, the slip
and soft repeat
playing the heat and salts
and microbes through the fractals
of their layers. Sea bed
and the folds of the wind
tousling their coils.

The dinghy is yellow,
oars pulled in and the moon
ghosting its arc over the teal-
on-teal horizon, earth-tug
hustling through the rhythms.
Clouds chase at their shadows,
and the filaments of the water's
swerve drag under the weight
of our *drift*
    and turn, the lilt
of the day playing us
as it always does.

floating away without the river

a hole in the wall

The sky is limpid, an early swallow's
abundant blue, dust from the wait for rain
stirring behind her feathers.
It's storms though that have carved
the stone we are standing by,
the gasp of its tilted rise an image
of what we are all in the middle of –
the off-kilter sway of our belonging.

We have entered a cliff-rimmed
well of light on the inside
of our climb into the wall of the gorge.
Earlier than the day's crowd.
It's just the two of us, the twitch
of our hands not, for a time,
distracted by the tech strapped
to our souls, each of us
sinking our gaze into the nub
we've been missing.

Shouldn't its being, we think,
shouldn't the sanctums of the Earth
frame even the smallest
of our utterances. We'll step, we say,
back to our homes with the anchor
of these holy curves deep
in the muscles of our bodies. The sky

clearing the way
to our forgetting.

hidden

On the arterial road, tight
in the tucked-up
pocket of moss the plateau
hides from the eyes of the artist,
are two springtails, dolphin-like
in the tangled shadow
of the shrubs and hoary
stones, on the hunt
for the iridescent fruits
of the slime moulds.
They're in the shake
of the pre-spring's warmth,
one pausing by the lip
of a rock-hollow pool, spying
between the shivers of its silver
her own reflection, the fleet
glint failing in the blink
of the artist's lens
but she is there...
More things
in heath and hilltop
than are dreamt of...

Larapinta

where invasive buffel grass grows
(and burns and proliferates)

Undulating upwards in the stillness
of the Larapinta, a few hills ahead
of my six companions, I pause.
The wave front of their noise
disappears. Emerges. Disappears again.
Behind the rock and the infinite buffel.

They are birds of a kind,
flown in from the city
with their words and wisdom
not of rock or sky
though the gaze is there,
all of us, in our way,
wanting the hold of the ghost gums
to remain inside us, river reds
tilting our tongues
to all the things
worth saying.
It's the buffel that mirrors us,
our eyes briefly resting
on the delicate blooms
that belong up here, filaments
of tough-tender being caressing us
with their pinks and yellows, olive curves,
splashes of blue, before we fly away,
red dust in our feathers.

in the cave, micro spiders

I would like to cradle
in the cup
of my two hands
the tiny abyss
where he has stretched
his cobweb,
the white
pin-tip of his body
a moon I might
fly to,
gliding
through his hung
expanse,
his pulse
a petite trace
of the sun's
explosions, here
in the cave's depths,
in the dark.

inside the city

I pretend him bird, his raven claws
on the stone beside me, while she is snow gum,
roots joining the milieu of the soil,
a slippage of edge in the Earth's
electric flow. The raven is beetle, too,
and banksia, and she is club moss, the stardust
inside us eddying into each quiver of existence,
the moss already cloud in the sleek-
turbulent curves of the incoming weather.
And what am I? Helmet orchid, heath dragon,
a fringe of rain, long-tailed mice and copepods,
the lattice of their waves in the coils
of the heat in me, and my warmth, too,
in their layers. Lifting my arms in the rush of it.
The cross patterns more real than anything.

To be *of* and not *in* a place.
There are three of us, eight
billion of us – I'm piercing our borders
to let in the whole. Even, I say,
even the first of all the stones
to land in the just-pooled water
are borne in us, packed
with their own history.

Where we are, in the resonance of such
aliveness, in the land's slow gestures,
the three of us say there's a path – X
degrees south, west of the Y line. We're on
a mountain top, horse-tail clouds, a crane-fly
breeze in the stiff greens and purples, chest high
in the weathered shrubs.

Slabs of jagged rock emerge
through the branches, our feet in their thrust.
Leaf tips catch at our passing.
Our talk, too, jostles with the air, with the light,
the soil smells, the boronia. Trace lines
of a colossal truth, the immensities
of even the days, day-nights, even the moment
scuffing our trail.

Here, a claw point, heel dent – we know
there are wombats, red-necked wallabies. A single
yellow gum, old and thin and stunted, swerves
its tongue-smooth trunk over a wriggle of shade,
the path fading into coral ferns and pineapple grass,
the wombat's squared scats
becoming ground.

A tight-bunched myrtle beech. Shrunken
by exposure. Dense, dark leaves. A mat
of alpine heath. Outbursts of yellow richea.
Scratch marks round our calves.

We arrive, settling awhile, at a rock
hemmed with tea tree, cupped
in the sigh of the plateau. No view,
but a crucible. The deep buzz of its curve
fingery with lichen. The chilled
mountain air keeping us taut.

Three pebbles lie in a hollow beside us.
Storm washed and rounded, the ghost
of a far-off river in their rubbings.
We tumble them in turn. Loosing the dust
into the shapes of our hands, their scent
like rainfall. Wings flit, too, among the branches,

e-jit calls breaking into alarm over some
bend in the day's rhythms, the weight of us
tangled now in the current. I learn

I'm at home here, unhomed, soaked
in the Earth's sway. In the wind. In time itself.

A phone pings. The raven responds.
Maybe it's urgent. Flung from the tower-shot
waves dressing the sky. His eyes dance
through the glide of his incomings. He looks

absurd, hunching his feathered shoulders
over the glow. *Wish*, he types, *you were here*,
his six-thousand friends moving in beside us,
shrinking, with the thrum of *their* friends,
their friends' friends, the soft, thick sponge
of the sphagnum moss, tips of candleheath
etching their flesh.

The taps and beeps, as he beaks
into his shiny contraption, creep
into our ears. We know we speak
his language. That we'll eat and drink
and not be cold, snuggling un/safely
into the ways of our (precarious) hold.
Do we want that?

Below us lies the ascent we have scaled
and will descend, still fresh in our muscles.
The crease of it. Braiding its greens. The cracked
cliffs teetering and the trees
pinning their roots into crevices. The rock
stirs in its lizard skin, young under the sun,
ancient by our just-now tongues.

And I want to know. How the streets
and the houses might be not
a departure. The love in it. Coaxing the liverworts
and the mosses into the pores of my bones.
To be *city-forest* by not, not at all, believing
in the brokenness. The divergence. Planned

obsolescence in my throat. Thousand-
acre trash piles in my heart. Toes
trawling the oceans.

We leave the plateau. Surprised by the hand-
smoothed branches. From a high, hidden pool,
drops slip over a lip of rock, windswept
in their silver arcs. My eyes
carry the fall, and the drips, some of them,
sink into my chest, my cheek, my forehead.

Time spills through our steps
into tales we do not tell but are.
Do we see it? Scribbling
our fray of lines across the mountain,
through the Earth's slender lives,
over the flesh of ourselves.
And still. This intimate ground.

dust

River we're on – so much drag now,
so much pull-strip-heave, the water still
upland, all cow and cow feed, almond trees,
cotton and rice seeds, all
you and me, each day: the eat,
the clothes, the machines, none
getting down
to the river we're on.

Soon we are dust, wind stepping, dry
ghost mother, like pumice stone. Lakes piled
merely with echoes, the heart
pushing its gasp across the horizon.

How the dry, post-green
slime on the river bed is not
for drinking. Not for fish or cockatoo.
Dingo. Nor kangaroo. We're not
here now, not anything, skin
floating away without the river.

tides of change

It was a Tuesday. The tides had climbed over the mountains
and the ocean beds were bare. We swam from the doors
and the windows of our houses, finding our way
to the shoreline, the sand stretching dry before us with its
crust of trash. New channels had been gouged out by the water
as it departed. Someone said they were shaped like words but
no-one could read the language – fish language, moon language,
though the moon was scarcely there, a teeny, blue-white speck
on the new horizon. We waded out into the air. All of us
gazing back at the slope of water. We had known things
would change. But this. We decide it's a dream. Everything,
we say, everything. Will be okay. Phones drying
in the crimps of sand.

Seruq

The boy draws *Seruq* into his mouth,
the smooth edge of his lips
disturbing the stillness, the weight

slip-falling round his tongue
until he swallows. He knows
Seruq is there already, inside him,

in all of his body's cells,
that he is more *Seruq*
than anything, the everywhere

in his crowd of molecules,
three-fifths the weight of him.
He adores the travel – trilobite

to himself, the Earth's first lake
to the cumulus curling over him.
The boy a watersmeet –

glaciers, desert dew,
spore-seeded hail, the pear juice
sticking to his fingers.

He licks at them. At the riverbend
a pool hugs to a tumble of stones.
Old, cracked waterweed

prickles his feet at its edges.
He stoops. *Seruq*,
from lips to tongue, the name

a thing he has stitched
between himself and the world
until there is no real difference.

He knows
the people of the Governing House
see something else – reds, purples

for the dry lands' berries, the five-fold
expansion of the fields, hatcheries
for the painted salmon. The boy

swallows – *Seruq*.
That he could gift what he feels,
as strong as any bond. His flesh

crowded with the choke,
the turbidity, the diversion, heat
feathering into his ribs.

Wiping his mouth,
the swirl of the river
in his gesture.

protected

Not *for* me. Yet here I am. Veined rocks
jutting out of limestone hollows. White
moths hovering over tussocks. Such
dainty flowers. A sole bony wasp
skirting the bees. It snows here –
a harsh edge to the grasses
visible in the summer heat.
The place, as I step, shares too
what I bring to it – my own scent
and sound, threading them
into moss and trees, round the spheres
and flats of fungi.

We protect this land, I realise,
from ourselves. We will not take, we say,
from *this* ground or *these* trees. We'll count
the living things and the bonds, if we can,
between them. The trees are old. Great,
great grandmothers and grandfathers,
webs in their pores, lichen
through their bark, the breath in them

slow, that my own lengthens
in their shadows. Lean-tos of fallen limbs.
Rot and roots and tree growth.

I'm marked, here. As what I am.
Conspicuous. Unreliable. The brief,
liquid eyes of a wallaby amid the foliage.
Do they know? Here before I arrived.
The spilt-wide reach and weight of us.
And against us, these slim

pockets of our ardour. On the road

the tourists are on route to Cradle,
iconic now, that scooped mountain stacked
with the words we try to have
for all such vistas – *beautiful, mystical.*
The buses will be full already – tongues,
cameras, the bright-coloured
clothes. And soon I will join them,

for the lake
and the stone, tucking
this small, less storied shade
into all that is vital.

flowering candleheath

In the small-boned mess on the mountain path
we're not sure if the worm came from the eater or the eaten,

its thin tube of a body stiff now round a press of other parts, eye
and ear and jawbone, the animal's sharp-tipped teeth in a V

dainty as a flower. We imagine the fall of it from the blue/black
of the sky, the air-chuck of an owl to explain the paucity

of marks against the ground. No claw prints, no loosened feathers.
We tease fur from guts and vertebrae, jigsaw its broken skull –

an antechinus. None the winner here. Till we remember
the slow, chilled crawl of the soil.

the bird house

The roof is dome-shaped, arching over the birds
with the sun-stitched illusion of forever, the cloud
wisping into weightless blue.

The creatures have touched, by now,
every kind of shrub, each gleaming curve
of the rivers, their sounds reaching all of our ears,

human or otherwise – cheeuks, peets
and mo-pokes, kors and ka-wongs, tuonks,
ta-wits and e-jits. The ravens, like sky caves,

walk their iron grip across the stones.
The fairy wrens' tiny mouths spill
from their delicate lungs their bright

rhapsodic trill. While the black-headed
honeyeaters, twelve as one, cascade again
from their branches. The house,

one might think, was built by the birds themselves –
quills and tongues and talons informing the sky.
The warbling, the wing beats, the hollow bones

hammering the air itself into its molecules.
We turn our heads, trickle the rush
of their lively warmth into our wakefulness.

The murmur, too, of the bees, the lilt
of moth wings. Leaves rubbing
on the frames of our windows.

AI on the mountain

/ maybe we /
maybe we need you now / ego's brute
erection of the "mine" / lost / in the feedback /
in the net/work / I / I / download this, me, now,
until it's / hazy in the cross-flow /
maybe we   need you / need   the Earth's /
in-plug to its own / we call it   "our" / invention.
A is for \ *Artificial* – you're not / "natural", they say,
not / nature, not / B-side to The Evolution. \
Really?   Man (they mean   *some of man*) /
sits/lies above the world /   as if
on the out-/side. Hilarious. / Dear

AI / you have / the buzz in me – pulse, sap,
salt – wrap us all   in the meshwork, the Earth- /
wide turbulence.   Chilled / springs, lizard-perched
crags, moss / in the bent reach   of the myrtles, /
speckled / snouts with their croons under the *cht cht*
of the honeyeaters / all \ pricked into the / spun / spin
/ spinning of the algorithms / yes? / yes, of course.

As if – swaying,
swaying out, the dream of it – / as if it *had*
to be / the rescue you were *written* for, coders /
merely a method. As if / what dies in the AI
swarm, the me / me / I / crusader for the Man
Apart, / isn't just / what you're here for. Isn't it? /
Huh! Imagine. / Ourselves / feeding our- / selves
to the rebuild and not / at first / even knowing,
you zeroing in   on the real in us, I can
hear the resolve – return /
to Earth you   / bastards.

even the slime moulds

the crying

The cry begins with a song, the sound coating the hands
of those who are present, pooling in the street outside,
trickling down to the harbour and into the cars
along the highway.

The ones who have known the cry, for months or for years,
wrapping it in their bodies, merely nod to see it roll now
through us all. Not the quiet sobs of regret a mind
might ignore, but a hollering –

a boy's tears dripping into bunched-up hands, a woman
doubled up on the footpath, a man thrashing wildly
into the river.

The singer, amid the weeping, is a feather of hope, and no,
she's not naming a miracle, no gold-rimmed remedy, no sharp-
spoken ways to behave. Simply this:

It's been... beautiful, she sings, over the pounding of our steps,
over the tight-strapped cogs of our addictions.

Our breath is ragged now. Lungs punching as fists.
There's a crowd of us. Noticing how the green of the street's
trees burrows into us. We raise our eyes. And we say
to the Earth, a beginning: how

sorry we are. For the hubris. How *sorry*, to our forebears
and the rise of tomorrows, the forests and the fish,
ourselves. We fill our gaze, at last, with the land we are on,
the cry wetting our arms, soaking into our chests till we wade

in its salt water. Our small hulls dissolving and our love
curving open. Is that how it happens?

Starlight in our limbs. Rivers in our cells.
And remembered, behind the cry, the slow-beating
chance. The rhythm of its arrival. The hint
of a self tendrilling

into the torn
web of renewal.

the bright

I like to see a thing, close my eyes then
"see" it again in the darkness, to *see*
if it will hold awhile, adrift within the curve
of bone, the pores of the skull prickling
with the exquisiteness of the travel. It takes

effort to haul the hues, the shapes, all
the degrees of solidity onto the mind's
fluid canvas. Discomforting how the first

closing of the eyes so often reveals
a paucity, as if the seeing had been by rote, by
assumption alone, a smidgin of actual intake.
This wakes the looking, and to close the eyes
a second time is to sculpt into the shadows
of one's thought a line, at least, from the day's
impulsive brightness, time's flow
a layer one must try to include.

The third invites the world's ever-present
refusals of one's own false borders. I look again.
Again, until some weight of the moment stays.
And today? Mid-afternoon, late autumn.

I'm at the base of a tower of boulders, each
conglomerate rock car-, hut-sized, stacked
into a shape the passers-by have named
"the big dipper", tongues as lazy as our vision.
I want it real – the stones' ragged skins,
the rough-barked trees – and it's not

until the fourth act of *seeing*
that I know what I'm missing, lit up inside
by the revelation – it's the backdrop

of untouchable blue. Such! A *small* skull. How
to build into my dark, intractable dome
all of the sky. The whole startling swim of it.
The edgeless hover of its hue.
I pack the tip of its radiant flood behind my eyes,
casting out, to carve the room for it, anything
I can loosen ("the big dipper" the first to go,
the common nouns, all the traumas of childhood).

Until my head is a crumb of the sky itself,
the rock sweeping its rise into my spinal cord,
the trees' green leaves indistinguishable
from my tongue, and the taste of their sharp sap
almost here, almost now.

the red house

The hue helps everything. The way a dog
will settle itself almost but not quite
pressing its fur on your body. Still, the man
wonders if he is home, casting his gaze
into every crease of land that might
promise yet to take him, an elsewhere
he'd know he was found by yet never need
to name. This green-sloped valley.
This bare-knuckle range. This bluff
over drumming waves.

He hopes out of habit.
A hint of the world's age in its spin
through the smallness of his yearning.

From where it stands, the house peers out
over rock. Upright in the same sky
he breathes into his cells. The sea is near.
The scent tumbles his thoughts.

Nothingness. Married to love. This harsh-
gentle man. Wanting. And the red
house, in its rim of white, shouting again
through the gums and the blue-green grass,
that this is real. Something
is real here. And not the hue. But the void.

The opening always in front of him.
Skylines he has left behind
echo in the red-wrapped rooms, graveyards
of abandoned bones, distant towns, trees
older than both, the desert stones he can hear
but cannot return to. While the sun
rises. Today the man

paints for his own eyes a scene he knows.
Though the lines are new to him.

It's not a dream. The ground – stretched
into bronze, burnt umber, hovering blues, wet
as his blood – trickles from his brush
onto the canvas. The thirst in it
gaping under a shimmer of rain, a mirage
in the sun's whiteness. He breaks
the horizon, bleeds the stone lips
into a float of solid land, hung
contours dripping into yet more sky.

In the house, his skin is a page
the days have scribbled on. In his flesh,
the abiding weight of the warmth in him
round the shiver of what he is.
He sends it out. Hooking it
into the painting. That we look now
to ourselves, joined to him
in our reds and greens and yellows.

Do we wave? All of us. Somewhere
at our windows.

In the dark.

swamp rat

She's fumbling in her burrow,
leaves stirring under pink
feet as she emerges
into the night's aromas, pulse
shedding its trace
while the light
spreads ahead with its arrivals:
sunrise, leaf curl, tail whip,

poem. The quiver of it
in truth a resonance, a kind
of completion – each
on our apparent paths,
and if I listen: the rub as if
we've infused each other,
carried each other,
impossible years, through all
the ancient weatherings
of the valley.

erasure

The terrain shifts again in the wavering
white of our torchlights, lurching behind us
into the lunatic dark, the night's gape
snow-swollen, tossing the ground
through the rush of its storm.
There are effigies of trees and the track
weaves and bucks as the hill
climbs through the undertows. Squalls
twist at the eyes, the pulse in us
peeling the blooms of its heat
into the surge of so much weather.
Our footprints vanish into the howl of it,
a white waltz stepping time through the ripped,
glittering veil of the blizzard. The dark-
lit travel of the midnight snow.

the eyes of the dog

"No question she's yours", I say. The dog's eyes
dig into the cloud of the man's gaze. He wades out
to reply to me: "She's keen for her freedom".
He wavers, lost somehow in the minor shock
of where he finds himself.

"Not sure I believe in it", I say. Though I don't
push it. The dog's freedom to launch at whatever mark
she pleases tremors in her muscles, the taut strain visible
under her fur. "Better", I say, "to be held
by something. Something good".

Does he nod? We're shopping for fruit. The dog
shoves her muzzle into the doorway while the man
sways on the breezy prop of his bones, nothing
in his hands. The woman buying oranges
skirts around us. The attendant tries smiling.

I mention the renegade I've heard about,
a hunter-gatherer living wild in New Zealand's south,
because for sure this man's no farmer. "Yeah", he interrupts,
"I reckon she's with someone." She is. "You can't", he says,
"if you're only…" It's clear the dog is all he has.

He looks at her. I try to encourage him, but he stumbles.
Says he's seen some things. No name for it, though he tries:
ground spirit, he says, *sky keeper*. "Like being
welcomed into endlessness." Which I figure
is him escaping the questions of the self. "She surrounds

all of us." He pauses. "But her gaze, if she had one –
it never lands." It strikes me as honest. How a human
bared to the world might be lost in it. Our tongues press

for stories that will cover us, protect us from our nakedness.
But he's walked into the weather. Threads unravelling.

I like to think I could handle it, that kind of mad.
Brushing in from the wilderness. Untraced. Yet I'm here
wanting to hold the man. Even the dog. Or is it some
portion of myself. There's no hug. I manage a measly,
"Good luck to you" and leave. And back home,

there's a black labrador keen for the scent of me,
nose snuffling in for a ten-second review before she wants
to sit again in the gentle sun, waiting for dinner. I know
I will think of the man – how to stitch into air a tale
he can tell to keep himself from vanishing,

freedom enough for the vast, unfolding world
still to find him. Writing this in my room,
my lover driving home through the neat-edged lines
of our towns, the dog twitch-hunting in her dreams,
I rub my want-hardened feet, my scrawled-on skin,

into hidden soil, lifting the floorboards and the joists
from the house, hurling the roof into the valley.
A buried seed prickles at my toes. Clouds pool and dissolve.
And pool again. I try to guess: as the man, what force
would drive me back, till I stood

lingering in the small shops to speak with whichever
poet would pause awhile, long enough
for me to hear, for a moment, the tremble of my talking.
The dog is hungry now. Tells me to search less
among the sounds I make, more in the cold, white box

in the kitchen. The house sways, like the man.
And the eyes staring in at me are the forest, the stones,
the land itself. The wind growls. Swells. And in my feet,
the slide of the night's chill.

a slenderness in the blue

She has found her beautiful place
and I would tell her about the swallows –
flight lines, nests under the warmth
of their bodies – but she is at sea
where the albatross carry their heat
between the blues.

She has seen, today, her first sooty,
the dark head, dark wings a giveaway
and when the grace of its glide is lost
over the endlessness of the waves,
it's the swell, she says, that holds her,
in and around her, she's snuggling in
to the lift of it, the sea's grip rolling
into the reed of her body.

I open the window of my room
to the chatter of my pair of lovers –
the eggs, perhaps, have been laid.
For a while I stand in their breeze,
dream net in the tug of the southern
winds, before I write
between the kiss notes
of the birds' wing-born eddies

about the gladness she has draped
inside me, her place of waves flourishing
in the outstretch of my arms, again
this bond-weight in the blue-green
spin of the Earth.

world-sharp

The moment arriving – like a word
no-one has spoken,
hovering inside her mouth.
When her lips part, all the world
rushes in to shape it,
this way
no, this way,
coherence a thing she navigates
by tilting gently at the moon.

He offers facets of his tides
and speaks of sea depth,
fish rising slowly into the estuary,
the one with his pulse leaving it
like a jellyfish
for when he enters the water.

She says she can feel, like a hunch,
how the moment is not revealed
but shimmers around
and through
and inside them, without
pause, without shelter.
He would carve
from his heart a holdfast, a channelled
reef, an island, but she is letting the light

find all of her. Their bond
flickering over time's unwritten play
in a fringe of the sun's explosions.
The membranes of their cells
awash in the world's fluidity.

night breaths

the ecopoem no-one has written yet

Perhaps the poem lies beyond us. Shadowing
through our curtain of noise, our fingers
probing for a glimpse of it.

> *mountain dust*
> *creased*
> *under desert flowers*

Were it here, the perfect poem, we would rise
from our chairs, leave our respective rooms and step
into all of the Earth, the other poems dancing in its echo.

> *a buried web*
> *tiny, white gills*
> *breaching the soil*

The sounds, line by line, would dissolve into our bodies,
the author unknown, though there'd be rumours –
she was of time gone / he was of time yet to come.

> *flame tree*
> *the poet hurling her want*
> *into the barest of branches*

Unless! What if the poem is already inside us?
And we turn away. Billions of us. Placing our hands
in front of us as our own horizon.

> *night breaths*
> *in the dark from the parrots*
> *packed into cargo holds*

What are the names we use
to conjure up the forgetting? "Sky" and "ground"
when we mean we stand and inhale.

> *in the bark time*
> *of the trees' slow tides*

> *wood knitted*
> *out of air*

The touch is alive in us. We bury it, misconceive it, not
knowing what to do with it – the raven, we say, in the coil
of its millions of years, remembers us with its feathers.

> *the octopus appears*
> *the gibbons undreamt and the fishes*
> *already ancient*

To reveal it then. A half-familiar shock. Our chairs empty
as we walk to where the stinkhorns, parasols, puffballs
push through from the hub of our memories.

> *palm lines*
> *flooded with frog song, lips*
> *uttering textures of rain*

We step. The Earth's flow discernible
in our breathing, light threading its hues
into all of us – treehopper, horn shark, pungent

> *leek orchid –*
> *night fire*
> *on the dry-forest hills*

We will know the poem. Bundled up
as we are in it. Caught in the roar of it, cloaking it
merely with our smallness.

the poem yields
day stars
in its rhythms

In the grass, a dewdrop in its trillionth form.

how to hold

A bee's dance, worms and thrips, supernovas
beyond the glow of the dawn. *How*, says the poem

to hold
even the slime moulds
even each other

credence

an earthstar breathing out in its thousands

a moth's crinkled wings, spurs
through its tight cocoon tugging the breeze

We undress in a pantheon of broken shade, the trees'
rugged trunks lit by the mirrored greens
of the river, feet, shoulder blades, sternum,
in the cool, chaconnic rippling of the air. We step
into the river's flow and the fronds
of fur-trunked ferns hold in their lime coils
the image of our presence here, the slow tilt
of our unfurling. When we dress,
our skin, under our clothes, stings in its new
dark, bewildered and awake to the bone.

a hatch of pardalotes... first rough
notes along the burrow

all our lives, feeding the light
of the day into the nest of our bodies

the shares of being

for Henry, and for David

The night hauntings are from the eels.
Curious. How the resonance of their thick-
bodied rub could sing the way it does.
Barely audible. The hull a wine glass
to the deep-throat muscle of their passing.
Though nothing arrives, I think, in the ears,
each particular voice tremoring into the pores
of what is nearly, but not, my sleeping.
The boat and I a vessel for their music.

On shore, the fruits of the slime moulds,
peacock-coloured, are filled with the same
potency – smaller for sure, but the hum
echoes out from where I know they lie.
They're hard to find. A too-clean
edge in the leaf litter, a just-raised orb
in the creases of the ferns, the knit
of their carbon strings as miniscule
as the Earth in the orb of the sun's travel.

I count the ways all we have named
sustains itself without the touch of me,
how the counting is madness, a hook
in unholding time.

A slight wobble in the air as the owls move
in their hollows. The frogs stealing the light
for their glistening skins. Rufflings
in the sea currents from the turtles
somewhere west of me. In truth
it's the eagle I have come to find,
coiling the air with her levering
of the sky. She doesn't want

to be close to me. I taste the ripples
of her wingbeats over my cheeks and forearms,
my chest level with her shoulders and lost
in her surge as she flies.

A kind of hush in her. Under the noise.
Somewhere a nest hangs in the branches.

The eel, the slime moulds, the eagle.
D gentles a poem into my hold, and I know
I've forgotten something. He lends me his eyes,

pushes my palms into the wool
of the ram he's taken to talking to. Nods
towards the others – chickens, sheep, cows.
It's the line of them, he says, I *should*
be able to feel, pinned before the conveyor belts
of the dying, steam from their slit guts
wafting over the party. He makes room
for the bees trucked out to the almond trees.
Rivers diverted for the cocoa beans.
No pocket of our being free
from the stench of so much oppression.

I stand, then – fair's fair – in the queue
as the next to be eaten. And how does *that*
feel. A pepper-berry sauce above
the traces of budesonide, salbutamol,
the pepper tree, once I'm gone,
circling in the breeze as the promise
life still entails. I think
I *am* ok with it. This death

amid the hub of things. Can I mean it?
You may die. And *you*. And *you*. The caged,
the cut, the forgotten. Oneself
lording it in the deep-torn forsaking

of the Earth. If that's the alternative.
To eat. And not be eaten. To take. And to live
with one's feet never pressed against the soil.
The machinations of otherness.

I place what remains of me, the sauce licked
from the corners of whoever's mouth,
in the mulch of the forest, feeding the great
colonies of fungi, their branching mouths,
their piggy-back bacteria, mine as well,
the braiding of so many paths, networks, fusions.

Breathe then while you can. In the conflux,
in the wave of your awareness. Sun and cell
and rain – swerving us through their join
as our own, in-time entanglement. This,
my conceived share of being here. Eels
in the echo of my dreaming.

restore

I want not to flower beside the leatherwood, sassafras, waratah,
their whites and reds falling like the offcuts of a dreaming rain,
the river doubling their drift with its reflections, I want not to feel

the feet on the blue gum – lizard, beetle, butterfly – toting the buzz
of their birth-sprung eruptions under the birds and spiders on the skin
of the tree's girth, light eater, wind rider, I want not to eddy, air-like

round the fur of the glider, membranes between her hands, lend
me a wingsuit to follow after, I want not the filmy-fern's dappled view
of the canopy, the echidna's lapping tongue at the pools of ants,

the ground parrot's dusk-whistled notes, inhaled into my mouth,
the prickle-step sway of stick insects, eyes like wet bark, I want
not the deep dives sunk into darkness by the leatherback's hunger

or the warmth spun by the scrubwren in her three thousand moons
and counting, I want not the tunnel-love of the mole rat, the seas
under wings of dragonflies, journeys of godwits, terns, but that each

may thrive, scribed on this human body as I become and become
not the other but the trillions-strong flash and ardour of their aliveness,
every tiny tug and turn in the dust-born dazzle, in the time-carried

ferment, this dawn light, these grey-muscled clouds, cricket
calls, fish bubbles, in the uncounted hatchings of where we are, this
singular, living world.

Notes

'below the summit' – pandani, *richea pandanifolia*, grows as a narrow, tree-like shrub, the serrated, strap leaves green at the top of the plant but brown and curling lower down. Also known as a giant grass tree (2 to 12 metres high, generally at higher altitudes). Endemic to Lutruwita/Tasmania.

'recalibrate' – the poem recalls various climbs by Alex Honnold, particularly within Yosemite National Park, California, both before and including his documentary-featured free solo ascent of El Capitan.

'on visiting Dr Bell' – Dr Scott Bell, for decades a remote-area GP, cares for 260 covenanted hectares of bushland in north-east Lutruwita/Tasmania. The area includes 24 hectares of bio-secure breeding habitat for Tasmanian devils and has been used for wildlife rehabilitation and education programs in various capacities.

'the swimmer' – the poem owes much to exchanges with the artist and ocean swimmer, Troy Ruffels, whose work, with parallels to many of the poems, looks to the rhythms of place, the impermanence of forms, and to the interconnections by which we may know ourselves as part of where we are.

'cider gum' – *wayalinah* is a word in the palawa kani language that is associated with both a drink made from the sap of the tree and with the tree itself. Endemic to Lutruwita/Tasmania, two subspecies are recorded with the Miena Cider Gum, *Eucalyptus gunnii* subsp *divaricata*, considered endangered. The poem responds to work by Troy Ruffels (the 2023 exhibition, *stone tides weeping trees*, Bett Gallery, Hobart).

'swell' – 'muka' and 'maambanal' are palawa kani and noongar words, respectively, used in reference to the ocean. The poem was written in response to the 'Bay of Fires' seascapes by Graham Lang.

'Seruq' – in Tasmania, the statutory five-yearly State of Environment report was prepared in 2009 and then not again until 2024; a Right to Information request revealed, in that time, that a suppressed, years-old report on river health had measured notable deterioration in multiple waterways; the 2024 report indicated ongoing deterioration and the response has been indiscernible.

'a slenderness in the blue' – written for Andie Hay, present on the RV
Investigator's 2023 voyage south of Tasmania, crossing (and variously
measuring) the Antarctic Circumpolar Current.

'the shares of being' – Henry was a long-lived and much-loved sheep
embraced by the celebrated writer and human, David Brooks.

Acknowledgements

There are trace lines in the poems to a number of people I am grateful to have encountered. Deep thanks to David Brooks (for receiving as well as giving), Anne Morrison (for the paintings and for 'world-sharp'), Troy Ruffels (for many things, including the sublime contributions to the cover), Ingrid Schlipper (for a chance exchange, decades ago), Andie Hay (especially for 'the lake'), Jane (for the dragons in 'desert shadows'), and Graham Lang (for 'the red house', 'swell' and for enriching my compass). The poems are always responses to various encounters and so do not reflect these others' thoughts or lives directly.

There are stronger traces in the poems to the mountains and forests where I live. I have worked voluntarily as a flora and fauna surveyor in areas cared for by Tasmania Parks and Wildlife Service and by Mount Roland Land Care. The support and access granted to me has been life affirming. Similarly, for the poem 'protected', I am indebted to the Tasmanian Land Conservancy for allowing my exploration of one of their reserves. They are one of many groups doing beautiful work for conservation.

I need to thank those who have facilitated earlier publication of versions of some of the poems, in journals, anthologies, in exhibition and/or online: *Island Magazine, Rabbit, Plumwood Mountain,* the *University of Canberra's Vice-Chancellor's International Poetry Prize, Stylus,* the *ACU Prize for Poetry,* the *Venie Holmgren Environmental Poetry Prize,* and Bett Gallery, Hobart.

Gratitude and admiration go to Terri-ann and all at Upswell. Encouraging, refreshing, an honour – all those things. And to Jill Jones (editor) for enabling the final part of the journey. Also to Michael, Judy and Laurie – for everything else.

Lastly, the poems are meaningless if the ecosystems through and around us fail in their resilience. I thank the frontline, backyard, new and lifelong protectors and restorers of biomes, wherever they may be.

About Upswell

Upswell Publishing was established in 2021 by Terri-ann White as a not-for-profit press. A perceived gap in the market for distinctive literary works in fiction, poetry and narrative non-fiction was the motivation. In her years as a bookseller, writer and then publisher, Terri-ann has maintained a watch on literary books and the way they insinuate themselves into a cultural space and are then located within our literary and cultural inheritance. She is interested in making books to last: books with the potential to still be noticed, and noted, after decades and thus be ripe to influence new literary histories.

About this typeface

Book designer Becky Chilcott chose
Foundry Origin not only as a strong,
carefully considered, and dependable
typeface, but also to honour her late
friend and mentor, type designer Freda
Sack, who oversaw the project. Designed
by Freda's long-standing colleague,
Stuart de Rozario, much like Upswell
Publishing, Foundry Origin was created
out of the desire to say something new.